YOUR DREAM IS NOT TOO BIG. IT'S THE RIGHT SIZE FOR YOU.

Date: ______

I see you, I feel you, I support you!

Date: ________________

I see you, I feel you, I support you!

IT TAKES COURAGE TO SHOW UP ON THE HARD DAYS. THANK YOU.

Date: ______________________

I see you, I feel you, I support you!

Date: ______________

I see you, I feel you, I support you!

YOUR PROGRESS MAY NOT BE AS MUCH AS YOU HOPED BUT YOU ARE MAKING AN IMPACT.

Date:

I see you, I feel you, I support you!

Date:

I see you, I feel you, I support you!

TAKE SOME TIME TO APPRECIATE YOUR BLESSINGS. THEY ARE MORE THAN YOU REALIZE.

Date: ______________________

I see you, I feel you, I support you!

Date:

I see you, I feel you, I support you!

TODAY, CHOOSE TO SMILE,
CHOOSE TO BE THANKFUL,
CHOSE TO CELEBRATE.
CHOOSE JOY!

Date: ______________________

I see you, I feel you, I support you!

Date: ______________

I see you, I feel you, I support you!

DON'T BE SO CONSUMED WITH WHAT ISN'T WORKING THAT IT OVERSHADOWS WHAT IS.

Date: ______________________

I see you, I feel you, I support you!

Date: ____________

I see you, I feel you, I support you!

SPEAK POSITIVELY OVER YOUR DAY. DON'T ALLOW NEGATIVE THOUGHTS TO FESTER.

Date: ______________________

I see you, I feel you, I support you!

Date: ____________

I see you, I feel you, I support you!

REMINDER: IT'S NOT TOO LATE, IT DOESN'T HAVE TO BE PERFECT, EVERY WALK IS DIFFERENT.

Date: ______________________

I see you, I feel you, I support you!

Date:

I see you, I feel you, I support you!

YOU ARE MORE CAPABLE THAN YOU THINK. YOU ARE VALUABLE, YOU ARE NECESSARY.

Date: ____________________

I see you, I feel you, I support you!

Date:

I see you, I feel you, I support you!

YOU ARE LOOKING FOR A WAY OUT BUT SOMETIMES THE WAY OUT IS TO GO THROUGH.

Date: ______________________

I see you, I feel you, I support you!

Date: ______________

I see you, I feel you, I support you!

THE BATTLES THAT YOU ARE FACING ARE HELPING TO BUILD ENDURANCE.

Date: ____________________

I see you, I feel you, I support you!

Date: ______________________

I see you, I feel you, I support you!

YOUR PURPOSE JOURNEY IS CALLING YOU TO LEAVE THE COMFORTABLE.

Date: ______________________

I see you, I feel you, I support you!

Date: ____________________

I see you, I feel you, I support you!

IT'S TIME TO STAND UP AND STAND OUT. IT'S TIME TO COME FROM THE BACK OF THE ROOM.

Date: ____________________

I see you, I feel you, I support you!

Date: ____________________

I see you, I feel you, I support you!

REST AND REJUVENATION ARE ALSO A PART OF YOUR PURPOSE JOURNEY.

Date: ______________

I see you, I feel you, I support you!

Date:

I see you, I feel you, I support you!

IT'S TIME TO FORGIVE AND
TO ASK FOR FORGIVENESS.
THE WEIGHT IS TOO MUCH.

Date: ______________________

I see you, I feel you, I support you!

Date:

I see you, I feel you, I support you!

CONSTANTLY RELIVING YOUR PAST SUCCESSES IS SLOWING DOWN YOUR FORWARD MOTION.

Date: ____________________

I see you, I feel you, I support you!

Date: ____________________

I see you, I feel you, I support you!

"NO" AND DISAPPOINTMENT HELP TO BUILD RESILIENCE. REJECTION IS HARD NOT FATAL.

Date: ______________________

I see you, I feel you, I support you!

Date: ____________________

I see you, I feel you, I support you!

TRY THE PHILIPPIANS 4:8 MIND DIET. IT DOES WONDERS FOR YOUR OUTLOOK AND MENTAL HEALTH.

Date: ____________________

I see you, I feel you, I support you!

Date: ____________

I see you, I feel you, I support you!

IT'S TIME TO RECOMMIT TO THE JOURNEY.

Date: ____________________

I see you, I feel you, I support you!

Date: ______________

I see you, I feel you, I support you!

IS THE CONSTANT COMPARING HELPING OR HURTING YOUR PURPOSE JOURNEY?

Date: ________________

I see you, I feel you, I support you!

Date: ______________

I see you, I feel you, I support you!

YOU DON'T HAVE TO
CARRY THE LOAD ALONE.
TRUST YOUR CIRCLE.

Date: ______________________

I see you, I feel you, I support you!

Date: ____________

I see you, I feel you, I support you!

YOU ARE NOT MEANT TO SIT AT EVERY TABLE. CHOOSE YOUR TABLES WISELY.

Date:

I see you, I feel you, I support you!

Date: ____________________

I see you, I feel you, I support you!

YOU ARE NOT FORSAKEN OR ABANDONED. YOU ARE NOT ALONE.

Date: ______________________

I see you, I feel you, I support you!

Date: ____________

I see you, I feel you, I support you!

CORRECTION IS UNCOMFORTABLE BUT VERY NECESSARY. IT IS A PART OF THE REFINING.

Date: ______________________

I see you, I feel you, I support you!

Date: ____________

I see you, I feel you, I support you!

ASKING FOR AND RECEIVING HELP DOES NOT MAKE YOU WEAK IT MAKES YOU WISE.

Date:

I see you, I feel you, I support you!

Date:

I see you, I feel you, I support you!

NOT EVERY GOOD OPPORTUNITY IS GOOD FOR YOU. IT'S OKAY TO DECLINE THE OFFER.

Date: ______________________

I see you, I feel you, I support you!

Date: ______________

I see you, I feel you, I support you!

SPREADING YOURSELF SO THIN IS MAKING YOU LESS EFFECTIVE.

Date: ____________________

I see you, I feel you, I support you!

Date: ____________________

I see you, I feel you, I support you!

ARE YOU BUSY WITH A PURPOSE OR ARE YOU USING BUSY TO AVOID YOUR PURPOSE?

Date: ______________

I see you, I feel you, I support you!

Date:

I see you, I feel you, I support you!

HOW MANY MORE APPROVALS DO YOU NEED TO BEGIN WALKING IN YOUR PURPOSE?

Date: ____________________

I see you, I feel you, I support you!

Date: ____________________

I see you, I feel you, I support you!

DON'T ALLOW FEAR OF THE UNKNOWN TO PREVENT YOU FROM FORGING NEW PATHS.

Date:

I see you, I feel you, I support you!

Date:

I see you, I feel you, I support you!

WHAT IS IN YOUR HAND RIGHT NOW? START WITH THAT.

Date: ____________________

I see you, I feel you, I support you!

Date: ____________

I see you, I feel you, I support you!

YOUR CALLING OR YOUR PURPOSE IS YOURS. NO ONE CAN TAKE IT FROM YOU.

Date: ______________________

I see you, I feel you, I support you!

Date: ______________

I see you, I feel you, I support you!

GIVE YOURSELF THE GRACE
THAT YOU SO WILLINGLY
GIVE TO OTHERS.

Date: ______________________

I see you, I feel you, I support you!

Date:

I see you, I feel you, I support you!

YOU ARE TAKING IN SO MUCH INFORMATION BUT IF THERE IS NO APPLICATION THEN YOU ARE JUST STORAGE.

Date: ______________________

I see you, I feel you, I support you!

Date: ____________________

I see you, I feel you, I support you!

YOU HAVE INVESTED SO MUCH TIME AND ENERGY BUT YOU HAVE TO MOVE ON. IT'S TIME TO PIVOT.

Date: ______________________

I see you, I feel you, I support you!

Date:

I see you, I feel you, I support you!

WHAT ARE YOU SAYING TO OTHERS AND YOURSELF ABOUT YOU? WATCH YOUR WORDS!!

Date: ______________________

I see you, I feel you, I support you!

Date:

I see you, I feel you, I support you!

YOUR TRUE CIRCLE WILL SUPPORT YOU BUT WILL ALSO HOLD YOU ACCOUNTABLE

Date:

I see you, I feel you, I support you!

Date: ____________________

I see you, I feel you, I support you!

HAPPY HOPE DAY!!! TODAY WE REMAIN OPTIMISTIC ABOUT OUR JOURNEY AND PURPOSE.

Date: ____________________

I see you, I feel you, I support you!

Date: ____________

I see you, I feel you, I support you!

GRATITUDE!
THANKFULNESS!
APPRECIATION!

Date: ____________________

I see you, I feel you, I support you!

Date: ____________________

I see you, I feel you, I support you!

KEEP MAKING THOSE POSITIVE CHANGES DON'T WORRY ABOUT THOSE WHO REFUSE TO SEE THEM.

Date:

I see you, I feel you, I support you!

Date: ______________

I see you, I feel you, I support you!

NO MORE HIDING OR DELAYING. YOU ARE UP, THIS IS YOUR TIME. SEIZE THE MOMENT!

Date: ______________________

I see you, I feel you, I support you!

Date: ______

I see you, I feel you, I support you!

WE ARE IN YOUR CORNER ROOTING FOR YOU. DON'T LET THE NAYSAYERS DISTRACT YOU.

Date: ______________________

I see you, I feel you, I support you!

Date: ______________________

I see you, I feel you, I support you!

THE NEED FOR PERFECTION IN EVERYTHING CAN BE A HUGE STUMBLING BLOCK.

Date: ______________________

I see you, I feel you, I support you!

Date:

I see you, I feel you, I support you!

CONSISTENCY! ESPECIALLY DURING THE HARD PARTS OF THE JOURNEY.

Date: ____________________

I see you, I feel you, I support you!

Date: ____________________

I see you, I feel you, I support you!

TAKE A MOMENT TO APPRECIATE WHAT YOU HAVE ACCOMPLISHED SO FAR AND GIVE THANKS.

Date: ____________________

I see you, I feel you, I support you!

Date:

I see you, I feel you, I support you!

RUN THE RACE THAT IS SET BEFORE YOU DON'T BE DISTRACTED BY SOMEONE ELSE'S RACE.

Date:

I see you, I feel you, I support you!

Date:

I see you, I feel you, I support you!

HAS CONSTANTLY DWELLING ON PAST MISTAKES, AND MISSED OPPORTUNITIES HELPED YOU?

Date: ______

I see you, I feel you, I support you!

Date: ______________

I see you, I feel you, I support you!

I KNOW YOU ARE LASER FOCUSED BUT DON'T FORGET TO CHECK ON YOUR CIRCLE.

Date: ______________________

I see you, I feel you, I support you!

Date: ____________________

I see you, I feel you, I support you!

TAKE A DEEP BREATH AND LET IT OUT SLOWLY. SAVOR THAT CUP OF COFFEE. QUIET THE NOISE.

Date: ______

I see you, I feel you, I support you!

Date: ______________

I see you, I feel you, I support you!

DON'T ALLOW THE DARK CLOUDS TO CONVINCE YOU THAT THE SUN WON'T EVER SHINE AGAIN.

Date:

I see you, I feel you, I support you!

Date:

I see you, I feel you, I support you!

NO JOURNEY IS FREE OF BUMPS AND OBSTACLES. YOU ARE NOT THE ONLY ONE FACING THEM.

Date: ______

I see you, I feel you, I support you!

Date:

I see you, I feel you, I support you!

MAKE SURE YOU ARE NOT JUDGING SOMEONE BASED ON YOUR PRIVILEGE.

Date: ______________

I see you, I feel you, I support you!

Date: ______________________

I see you, I feel you, I support you!

YOU ARE LOOKING FOR SOMETHING BIGGER BUT YOU MAY ALREADY BE WALKING IN YOUR CALLING.

Date:

I see you, I feel you, I support you!

Date:

I see you, I feel you, I support you!

IT'S EASIER TO SHARE THE WINS BUT THERE ARE LESSONS TO SHARE IN THE LOSSES TOO.

Date: ______________________

I see you, I feel you, I support you!

Date: ______________

I see you, I feel you, I support you!

TAP INTO THOSE GIFTS AND TALENTS THAT HAVE BEEN LAYING DORMANT WITHIN YOU.

Date: ______________________

I see you, I feel you, I support you!

Date: ______________________

I see you, I feel you, I support you!

NO OPPORTUNITY IS GREATER THAN YOUR INTEGRITY. YOUR CHARACTER MATTERS.

Date: ______________________

I see you, I feel you, I support you!

Date:

I see you, I feel you, I support you!

FANTASIZE!
VISUALIZE!
ACTUALIZE!

Date: ______________________

I see you, I feel you, I support you!

Date:

I see you, I feel you, I support you!

BE A GOOD STEWARD OF EVERYDAY THAT YOU ARE BLESSED TO SEE.

Date: ______________________

I see you, I feel you, I support you!

Date:

I see you, I feel you, I support you!

YOU CAN ADMIRE OTHERS BUT YOU HAVE TO FULFILL YOUR PURPOSE AS YOUR AUTHENTIC SELF.

Date: ____________________

I see you, I feel you, I support you!

Date: ______________

I see you, I feel you, I support you!

GOD WILL PROVIDE EVERYTHING THAT YOU NEED FOR THE DAY THAT YOU ARE IN.

Date: ______________________

I see you, I feel you, I support you!

Date:

I see you, I feel you, I support you!

THE WAY THAT YOU ARE LIVING IS A REFLECTION OF WHAT IS IN YOUR HEART. (PROVERBS 27:19)

Date:

I see you, I feel you, I support you!

Date:

I see you, I feel you, I support you!

ON THOSE DAYS WHEN YOU ARE FEELING WEARY OR UNMOTIVATED REMEMBER YOUR WHY.

Date:

I see you, I feel you, I support you!

Date: __________

I see you, I feel you, I support you!

DON'T BE SELECTIVE WITH YOUR COMPASSION.

Date:

I see you, I feel you, I support you!

Date:

I see you, I feel you, I support you!

GIVE YOUR MIND A BREAK.
THE OVERTHINKING IS
EXHAUSTING.

Date: ______________________

I see you, I feel you, I support you!

Date:

I see you, I feel you, I support you!

ARE YOUR RESPONSES BASED ON WHAT IS ACTUALLY HAPPENING OR WHAT YOU CREATED IN YOUR HEAD?

Date:

I see you, I feel you, I support you!

Date: ____________________

I see you, I feel you, I support you!

ALL OF THE HARD WORK THAT YOU HAVE PUT IN WILL YIELD FRUIT.

Date: ______________________

I see you, I feel you, I support you!

Date:

I see you, I feel you, I support you!

YOU HAVE A BOOK FULL OF IDEAS. PICK ONE!

Date: ______________________

I see you, I feel you, I support you!

Date:

I see you, I feel you, I support you!

YOU WERE NOT OVERLOOKED. GOD IS ORDERING YOUR STEPS. TIMING IS EVERYTHING.

Date: ______________________

I see you, I feel you, I support you!

Date: ______

I see you, I feel you, I support you!

KEEP EVERYTHING IN PERSPECTIVE. ONE MISSTEP DOES NOT MAKE YOUR WHOLE LIFE A FAILURE.

Date: ______________________

I see you, I feel you, I support you!

Date: ______________

I see you, I feel you, I support you!

HAVE A WONDERFUL DAY
ON PURPOSE.

Date: ______________________

I see you, I feel you, I support you!

Date: ______________

I see you, I feel you, I support you!

IS FEAR CAUSING YOU TO
REMAIN WHERE YOU ARE?

Date: ______________________

I see you, I feel you, I support you!

Date: ____________

I see you, I feel you, I support you!

Motivation Moments

PERSONAL & PROFESSIONAL GOALS

My Goals:

My Why:

Action Step 1:

Action Step 2:

Deadline:

PROGRESS & REFLECTIONS

I see you, I feel you, I support you!

Motivation Moments

PERSONAL & PROFESSIONAL GOALS

My Goals: ______________________________

____

____

My Why: ______________________________

____

Action Step 1: ______________________________

____

Action Step 2: ______________________________

____

Deadline: ______________________________

PROGRESS & REFLECTIONS

____

____

____

____

____

____

____

____

____

I see you, I feel you, I support you!

Motivation Moments

PERSONAL & PROFESSIONAL GOALS

My Goals: ______________________________

____

____

My Why: ______________________________

____

Action Step 1: ______________________________

____

Action Step 2: ______________________________

____

Deadline: ______________________________

PROGRESS & REFLECTIONS

____

____

____

____

____

____

____

____

____

I see you, I feel you, I support you!

Motivation Moments

PERSONAL & PROFESSIONAL GOALS

My Goals: ______________________

____

____

My Why: ______________________

____

Action Step 1: ______________________

____

Action Step 2: ______________________

____

Deadline: ______________________

PROGRESS & REFLECTIONS

____

____

____

____

____

____

____

____

____

I see you, I feel you, I support you!

Motivation Moments

PERSONAL & PROFESSIONAL GOALS

My Goals: ______________________________

____

____

My Why: ______________________________

____

Action Step 1: ______________________________

____

Action Step 2: ______________________________

____

Deadline: ______________________________

PROGRESS & REFLECTIONS

____

____

____

____

____

____

____

____

____

I see you, I feel you, I support you!

Motivation Moments

PERSONAL & PROFESSIONAL GOALS

My Goals:

My Why:

Action Step 1:

Action Step 2:

Deadline:

PROGRESS & REFLECTIONS

I see you, I feel you, I support you!

Motivation Moments

PERSONAL & PROFESSIONAL GOALS

My Goals:

My Why:

Action Step 1:

Action Step 2:

Deadline:

PROGRESS & REFLECTIONS

I see you, I feel you, I support you!

Motivation Moments

PERSONAL & PROFESSIONAL GOALS

My Goals: ______________________________

____

____

My Why: ______________________________

____

Action Step 1: ______________________________

____

Action Step 2: ______________________________

____

Deadline: ______________________________

PROGRESS & REFLECTIONS

____

____

____

____

____

____

____

____

____

I see you, I feel you, I support you!

Motivation Moments

PERSONAL & PROFESSIONAL GOALS

My Goals:

My Why:

Action Step 1:

Action Step 2:

Deadline:

PROGRESS & REFLECTIONS

I see you, I feel you, I support you!

Motivation Moments

PERSONAL & PROFESSIONAL GOALS

My Goals: ______________________________

My Why: ______________________________

Action Step 1: ______________________________

Action Step 2: ______________________________

Deadline: ______________________________

PROGRESS & REFLECTIONS

I see you, I feel you, I support you!

Motivation Moments

PERSONAL & PROFESSIONAL GOALS

My Goals:

My Why:

Action Step 1:

Action Step 2:

Deadline:

PROGRESS & REFLECTIONS

I see you, I feel you, I support you!

Motivation Moments

PERSONAL & PROFESSIONAL GOALS

My Goals: ______________________

____

____

My Why: ______________________

____

Action Step 1: ______________________

____

Action Step 2: ______________________

____

Deadline: ______________________

PROGRESS & REFLECTIONS

____

____

____

____

____

____

____

____

____

I see you, I feel you, I support you!

Motivation Moments

PERSONAL & PROFESSIONAL GOALS

My Goals: ______________________________

____

____

My Why: ______________________________

____

Action Step 1: ______________________________

____

Action Step 2: ______________________________

____

Deadline: ______________________________

PROGRESS & REFLECTIONS

____

____

____

____

____

____

____

____

____

I see you, I feel you, I support you!

Motivation Moments

PERSONAL & PROFESSIONAL GOALS

My Goals:

My Why:

Action Step 1:

Action Step 2:

Deadline:

PROGRESS & REFLECTIONS

I see you, I feel you, I support you!